P9-AFY-881

The World of Work

Choosing a Career in
Hotels, Motels, and Resorts

Hotels, motels, and resorts offer a variety of career opportunities, from front desk clerk to manager to owner.

The World of Work

Choosing a Career in Hotels, Motels, and Resorts

Nancy N. Rue

HAVANA PUBLIC
LIBRARY DISTRICT
201 West Adams Street
Havana, IL. 62644 98-708

J
647.94
Rue

THE ROSEN PUBLISHING GROUP, INC.
NEW YORK

Published in 1997 by The Rosen Publishing Group, Inc.
29 East 21st Street, New York, NY 10010

Copyright © 1997 by The Rosen Publishing Group, Inc.

All rights reserved. No part of this book may be reproduced in any form without permission in writing from the publisher, except by a reviewer.

First Edition

Library of Congress Cataloging-in-Publication Data

Rue, Nancy N.
    Choosing a career in hotels, motels, and resorts / Nancy N. Rue.
       p.   cm.—(The world of work)
    Includes bibliographical references and index.
    ISBN 0-8239-2273-1
    1. Hospitality industry—Vocational guidance. I. Title. II. Series.
TX911.3. V62R84   1996
647.94′023—dc20   96-9450
                                         CIP
                                         AC

Manufactured in the United States of America

Contents

Introduction

Jim, a hotel manager, looked across his desk at Anita, the young woman he was interviewing. She was nineteen and had graduated from high school two years ago. Although she had worked at several office and retail jobs since then, she stated on her job application that she was ready to begin a "real career."

After carefully reading her neatly written job application, Jim looked up at Anita. He asked, "Why do you want to work here? Why do you want a job in a hotel?"

"I've held several different jobs since I was sixteen," Anita said, "but my favorite one was a job I had this past summer when I worked as an assistant desk clerk in a motel my aunt manages. It was exciting because I faced all kinds of different situations, and I had the chance to meet new people every day. I learned a lot about motels on the job."

"Sounds like the job did a lot for you," Jim said. "What did you do for it?"

Anita thought for a moment. "You need to have a bright personality and the desire to make people comfortable if you're going to work in a motel," she said. "My work experience made me realize that I have these qualities. I found that I was able to gain our guests' trust by interacting with them in a friendly way."

Jim thought Anita was just the person he would like to hire for his hotel. She obviously liked people, and she was full of enthusiasm. Most importantly, she had what he called a "service attitude." She could help create an environment that guests would appreciate and remember because she seemed to know how to make people feel comfortable.

"I think it's a good choice," Jim told her. "In the lodging industry—which includes hotels, motels, and resorts—we're expecting that by the year 2000 there will be well over 500,000 new entry-level positions. And these jobs offer excellent opportunities to advance to higher-level positions."

Anita grinned at him. "I've read that in less than ten years, travel and tourism together will be the country's number one employer. One out of every five workers in the United States will be in this field."

A positive service attitude is essential in the lodging industry. You must be willing and able to help every customer with a friendly smile.

Jim was impressed. "You've done your homework," he said. "You're exactly the kind of employee the lodging industry needs. I'd like to offer you the job."

As Anita thanked him and left his office smiling, Jim remembered when he had been in Anita's shoes—a young person looking for a job with some real career opportunities. He had started working at age thirteen washing dishes in a local hotel restaurant. He had worked his way up to the position of bellhop his last summer before college. To help pay for college, Jim worked as a night clerk at the front desk of the College Inn. He had liked this job so much

*that he decided to major in hotel management.
By the time he was twenty-seven, he was
running a motel with 107 rooms. Because Jim
had always been willing to try new ideas and
had a positive service attitude, his motel had
been a huge success. When he found out about
a hotel manager position in a larger city, he'd
been able to show through his experience and
education that he was the best person for the
job.*

Jim is living proof that the lodging industry
is one in which you can rise through the ranks
to the top position of hotel general manager.
Many general managers have started working at
the bottom the same way he had.

Opportunities in the Lodging Industry

The top twenty-five lodging chains in North
America offer about one million jobs. If you
include the many smaller lodging chains and
the hundreds of independent hotels, the
number of workers in the industry becomes
incredible. A wide range of opportunities exist
for young people like Anita.

With an *entry-level* job in any area of the
industry, new employees are offered a good
salary. They also have a good chance of being

You may choose to work in the food and beverage division of a hotel. If so, you may be the one to decide what the dining room will serve.

promoted to a higher-level position rather quickly. The lodging industry offers more jobs than any other field except health care.

There are many different entry-level positions in which you can start your career in the lodging industry. Perhaps you are interested in the *management* of a hotel. You could assist the general manager with administration and be involved in the operation of the hotel. This may include interacting with employees and guests and maintaining budgets.

Or you might be more interested in helping with the hotel's *food and beverage division*. That would involve working with menus, linens, uniforms, and the dining room decor. You would also participate in booking events like banquets and conventions.

A person with poise and personality might find that the *rooms division* is a good place to begin. In the *front office* you would deal with room occupancy, filing systems, correspondence, reservations, and keeping in touch with the other departments in the hotel. In the *guest services division* you would be handling the needs of guests with courtesy and efficiency even when they had complaints or special requests. *Housekeeping, laundry*, and *uniformed services* (such as the bellhops) are options, too. Some people don't consider these divisions because they don't think that they are glamorous. In fact, they are a great place to break into the lodging industry.

In the *accounting* department you would be handling the hotel's money and its income and expenses.

If you wanted to work in *sales* you would be involved in making sure that the hotel had plenty of guests by meeting with international, national, regional, and state organizations and travel agents. Salespeople go to conventions in other cities and advertise the hotel's facilities and services to increase business.

You may enjoy the *convention* aspect of hotel operation. You could help coordinate conventions, meetings, and banquets, develop menus, and take care of any problems that crop up.

Engineering is also an important part of the lodging industry. Hotels always need people to work on such trades as refrigeration, heating, plumbing, roofing, and maintenance to keep the building operating.

There are many more areas of the hotel business that you could go into. These include dealing with employees by working in the *personnel* office, s*ecurity*, *recreational facilities*, and *public relations*.

Whatever path you decide to take in the lodging industry, you will probably have a challenging job with the opportunity for promotions. Most people who start a career as a hotel professional never want to leave it.

Questions to Ask Yourself

The field of hotels and motels offers a great selection of possible jobs. 1) What are some of the fields of work involved in the hotel/motel industry? 2) If you were hired, into what field would you hope to be promoted eventually? 3) What is a service attitude?

The service a customer receives from a valet may set the tone for the
customer's entire stay.

At Your Service

1

If you pull up a car to the Maui Marriott Resort in Hawaii, Mark or one of the eighteen valets he supervises will greet you and park your car. Mark and his crew park and retrieve cars for all hotel guests at one of Hawaii's most exclusive resorts. Mark and his valets also greet new arrivals, unload their luggage, and control traffic in the hotel's driveway. The crew must be welcoming, courteous, and ready to answer any questions that guests may ask when they first arrive.

Mark started off in the hotel business at a smaller hotel. There he worked as a bellhop. The wages were low, but he earned up to $100 a day in tips during the busiest season. He quickly learned that there was more to the job than just helping people with their luggage. He needed to be able to help them with travel problems or to suggest where to go or what to see on their vacation. He always had to be available and friendly.

He also learned a lot about the hotel business from other employees. After four years, he was promoted to the position of bell captain.

When Mark heard about the Maui Marriott Resort, he saw a chance to become part of an international hotel chain. He applied for the bell captain position. He was hired instead as parking valet captain. Because it was a new hotel, Mark was asked to write job descriptions for himself, his valets, and his cashiers. He helped interview some of the valet applicants and train new valet staff members. Mark has a lot of responsibility. He likes his work. What he enjoys most is meeting people from all over the world and the opportunities for advancement.

The Valets

As a *valet*, you can set the tone for a guest's entire visit. Valets must report to work on time in full uniform and wear a name tag. When a car pulls up, the valet opens the door, greets the client, unloads the luggage, and parks the car in the hotel parking lot. Before locking the car, he or she checks to see that the lights, wipers, and radio are turned off.

The valet then returns to the valet desk and turns the key over to the cashier. The cashier stores it on a rack with an identifying tag. When a guest wants to use his or her car, the valet gets the key from the cashier and drives the car up to the entrance for the guest.

Valets have to follow certain rules while driving other people's cars. These include observing speed limits, having a valid driver's license, and providing a driving record every six months showing any tickets, accidents, or arrests. Valets should also keep parking lots and driveways clean and have a basic knowledge of the area including its history, people, and attractions.

Hotels often have their own vehicles available for guests. Valets keep them clean and well-serviced.

As a *parking valet captain* like Mark, you would supervise the valets and park and retrieve cars. This would give you the opportunity to earn tips to add to your wages. You would also be responsible for scheduling the valets' work shifts and for managing the department's payroll.

Felicia, Front Desk Clerk

When a guest checks in at the Downtowner Motor Hotel, Felicia gives her a set of room keys and a friendly welcome. As the front desk

Front desk clerks check people in and out of the hotel.

clerk, her main responsibilities are taking reservations, registering guests, keeping track of room charges, and answering the phone. It is also important for her to give guests whatever help she can.

Felicia dropped out of school as a teenager. She later passed the general educational development, or GED, tests by attending night school. Felicia recommends that you stay in high school if you want to work in the hotel/motel business. She also suggests taking courses in psychology, accounting, bookkeeping, computers, math, and typing.

Felicia has worked as a front desk clerk at the Downtowner for seven years. She was recently told that she will soon be promoted to office manager and reservations agent.

Felicia arrives at the 131-room motel at 6:30 A.M. She counts the cash in the till and keeps an ongoing record of money transactions. She prepares the deposit for the safe. She then takes over the phone and the front desk. Mornings are busy with people checking out and paying their bills. She completes a form for each guest who checks out. She also has to check for any additional charges such as phone calls. When people check in, Felicia fills in all the necessary paperwork and makes sure it is properly filed. She assists people in making reservations as well.

Felicia knows that if she ever has to move, she won't have any trouble finding a job as a desk clerk because her fine communication skills are in demand. This position is seeing faster than average growth because more hotels and motels are being built.

The Front Desk Clerk

The position of *front desk clerk* is extremely important. Sometimes the desk clerk must

Bellhops earn tips as well as a salary. A friendly, helpful bellhop can earn a good amount of money in tips.

deal with guests who are upset because the faucet drips or the people next door are noisy. No matter what the complaint, in the hotel business, the customer is always right.

As a front desk clerk, you get to deal with the public. You work in an environment in which the goal is not only to make money. You also make each guest's stay a happy and comfortable one. You spend time with the guests. You sometimes help them in difficult situations. In this way, you become friends with many people, especially those who come back often.

Carlos, Bellhop

Guests who arrive at the Airport Hilton in Jacksonville, Florida, between 5:00 P.M. and midnight may be greeted by Carlos. Carlos, a bellhop, will take their luggage to their room. He may even have driven them to the hotel from the airport in the hotel van.

Carlos has been working at the Hilton for a year. In addition to his main duties, Carlos helps guests with personal requests. He assists them with dry cleaning and brings them irons, ironing boards, and hair dryers. He also escorts visitors on tours of the hotel, helps with valet parking, delivers hotel mail to the post office, and makes sure the lobby is tidy.

Carlos recommends that you take courses in psychology and sociology as well as in speech and communications if you want to go into the lodging industry.

Carlos has chosen to work the night shift so he can go to college during the day. He also attends monthly staff meetings to keep up-to-date on the hotel's new services and plans.

The Bellhop

A *bellhop* wears a uniform, which his employer provides and cleans for him. On a typical day a bellhop checks in at the employee lounge. He makes sure his appearance is neat before he goes into the lobby. He inspects the lobby for trash. He then checks the clipboard at the bellhops' station for any events, such as banquets or meetings, scheduled at the hotel.

A bellhop might drive guests to the airport with the hotel van. He might also be responsible for making sure that the hotel's van is serviced for the next day.

At the end of his shift, a bellhop writes out guest requests for the bellhops working the

A maid's duties vary according to the type of hotel, motel, or resort he or she works in. Some places may require a maid to turn down the sheets on a guest's bed, place mints on a guest's pillow, or even run a bath for a guest.

next shift. He then turns in his keys to the desk clerk.

Some bellhops say the worst part of the job is having to deal with the occasional impatient guest. But rude guests can usually be handled with a sense of humor. For the most part, the people a bellhop meets are courteous and friendly. Most bellhops receive health insurance, a paid vacation, and discounts at the hotel. Bellhops are often promoted to front desk clerks. They can continue to advance from that position. Although bellhops

work for minimum wage, they also receive tips
of up to $100 a day.

Kim, Maid

*Kim didn't finish high school, so the jobs
open to her in Virginia Beach were limited.
She had enjoyed taking home economics
courses in school, so she applied for a job as a
maid at an eighteen-room motel. Although the
pay was low and the tips were small, she gained
enough experience there to land a better-
paying maid's job at the Holiday Inn a year
later.*

*She trained with an experienced Holiday
Inn maid for a week. She was then ready for
her job assignment cleaning eighteen of the
eighty-four rooms each day during the peak
season and twelve in the off-season. The more
rooms she cleans the more she is paid.
However, she still has to be thorough. Often the
head housekeeper checks up on the maids to
see if they're doing a good job. The job of maid
involves vacuuming, dusting, changing the
linens, cleaning the bathroom, and putting out
fresh towels and supplies for guests. On top of
her regular pay, she also earns tips from most
guests. She can earn around $150 a week just in
tips.*

The worst part of the job, according to Kim, is having to clear the messes that many guests leave. The best part has been her recent advancement to the laundry facility. There she washes, dries, and folds towels, sheets, and pillowcases. While the laundry is washing and drying, Kim is allowed to read a book.

Every other Sunday, she also acts as housekeeper. In this position, Kim cleans rooms, assigns the other maids the rooms they will clean, and checks on rooms cleaned by new maids before guests arrive. At the end of the day, she also makes sure that all the cleaning and supply rooms are properly locked. As housekeeper, Kim is given an extra two hours' pay for her added responsibilities.

Kim does her job well and hopes to be promoted to the position of head housekeeper.

The Maid

Maids are often provided with accident and life insurance. They may receive a Christmas bonus and a week of paid vacation each year.

In return for these benefits, Holiday Inn and other hotels ask that a maid do a thorough job and treat guests with patience and courtesy.

Other Opportunities in the Service Areas

Mark, Felicia, Carlos, and Kim all work in the *service areas* of the lodging industry. Hotels have always offered many opportunities for the young or those without specialized skills. The positions of housekeeper, clerk, bellhop, and valet are examples of these opportunities. They can all lead to advancement. They all have flexible hours for the person who wants to continue his or her education.

The jobs that have been discussed so far are only a few of those available in the service areas. If we divide a hotel into the *front-of-the-house*, where employees are highly visible to the guests, and the *back-of-the-house*, where they are not, we can see many other opportunities.

Front-of-the-House

The staff of the *front office* includes room clerks, rack clerks, mail clerks, information clerks, reservations clerks, telephone operators, secretaries, and concierges.

In the *service department* there are baggage porters, lobby porters, doormen, bellhops, checkroom attendants, valets, and garage attendants.

Doormen are a part of the front-of-the-house staff.

The front-of-the-house also includes the sales and accounting departments, which will be discussed in the next chapter.

Back-of-the-House

The *food preparation* department includes the chef, fry cook, roast cook, vegetable cook, pastry cook, salad person, baker, butcher, and kitchen steward, as well as pantry people, food and wine stewards, and dishwashers.

Food service includes waiters and waitresses, hostesses, room service waiters, bartenders, and busboys.

In addition to maids, *housekeeping* is staffed by linen room people, laundry people, and window washers. Housekeeping employs 10 to 15 percent of the total work force of a hotel.

Engineering and maintenance requires the services of air-conditioning and refrigeration engineers, carpenters, electricians, plumbers, and painters.

Starting salaries for these jobs are often minimum wage or slightly higher. Some jobs pay lower wages than others, but many of these will also allow you to earn tips. In addition, uniforms are usually free. Some jobs include meals while on duty and discounts at other hotels in the chain you work for.

Resort hotels offer their own benefits, such as the chance to live in a new place with a particular climate. Many employees enjoy working in an area where many people go on vacation such as the Caribbean or Hawaii.

There is a lot of contact with guests in all of these jobs. This makes them excellent training grounds for higher-level positions and fun and challenging in themselves.

Questions to Ask Yourself

A hotel or motel must fill many positions, ranging from maid to general manager. Promotions are frequent for hard-working employees. 1) What is the "front-of-the house"? 2) What is the "back-of-the-house?" 3) What are the service areas of the hotel/motel industry?

Down to Business

2

Many aspects of running a hotel or motel are handled in the *business office*. These aspects include *finance, sales, publicity,* and *personnel.* These kinds of jobs exist in almost every type of business. But the excitement that surrounds them in a hotel or motel and the chance for advancement make them more attractive to a lot of people.

Money, Money, Money!

It takes a lot of money to run a hotel and a lot of time to keep track of it. For this reason, a hotel's financial department plays an important part in the way the hotel operates.

The *controller* supervises all the employees who handle money. The bigger the hotel, the more employees the controller has to supervise. The controller is assisted by *clerks*.

The *accounting department* also uses clerks. The *accountant* and his staff deal with all the hotel's accounts, from charges for room service to the purchase of new bedsheets to the payment of the hotel's employees. The *cost accountant* is responsible for the hotel's recordkeeping. The *credit manager* monitors all of the hotel's credit procedures. He or she makes sure that the hotel's policies are followed and that new accounts are set up properly.

The *accounts receivable supervisor* is in charge of the accounts receivable department. If someone owes the hotel money, he and his staff handle it. If the hotel owes money, the *accounts payable supervisor* and her staff take care of it. All of these jobs could lead an employee to the position of *assistant controller* and then to controller.

Have I Got a Deal for You . . .

A hotel has no money to handle if guests don't check in at the front desk. That's why most hotels need a strong *sales* and *marketing* force to increase business. The *director of marketing and sales* manages a team of *sales managers*. *Marketing assistants* do research for the director and the sales associates.

It is the responsibility of the sales department to sell what the hotel has to offer— rooms, convention space, and services. This involves meeting people from all over the world and representing the hotel to them in a positive way. As a result, the competition for these jobs is stiff.

To work in sales, you have to enjoy competition, be able to spend several hours on the phone each day, and work under the pressure of a *quota*. A quota is the number of sales you have to make in a certain period of time. You must also be willing to travel and be away from your family, as well as come to work early and stay late.

When business threatens to slow down, people who work in marketing and sales start brainstorming about ways to persuade more guests to come to the hotel. This may involve things like price cuts, free breakfasts, discounts on golf or skiing, two-for-one deals, and air-and-lodging packages. If you can come up with creative ideas, sales might be for you.

The People Side

The *personnel* or *human resources department* is responsible for hiring and firing the hotel's employees and for keeping workers happy and satisfied.

The *personnel manager* oversees the department. She works with the *training manager.* He is in charge of the hotel's management training program. This program prepares employees for positions like *assistant personnel* or *training coordinator.* The *benefits coordinator* handles employee *benefits*, such as health insurance. The *employee relations manager* deals with the rights of the hotel workers. These jobs are important because if the people who run the hotel are happy and have good working conditions, they will do their jobs efficiently.

Getting Training

Career counselors and hotel executives recommend that people who are interested in the business side of the lodging industry attend a hotel school. In addition, most hotel chains offer management training programs. Here trainees can either rotate among all the departments or can spend six months in one special area. Many of these trainees come from major hotel schools. They are often recruited by the hotels themselves. A trainee can expect a salary in the $20,000 range at the end of the program.

If you've worked in any area of the hotel industry but have *not* gone to a hotel school, you can still qualify for an entry-level job.

In the hotel business, experience is valuable. The hotel industry offers many opportunities for those interested in a hotel career. Summer positions for non-managers are often available. Some hotel sales departments have summer internship programs for students. There they can learn market research, computers, and how to organize sales projects. Internships don't pay very much, but they offer you a chance to get your foot in the door.

Some hotel executives suggest that if you can't get into the department in which you're interested, take the first available job. Then let the people around you know what your goals are. Managers will remember you when a position opens up if you've done a good job.

Questions to Ask Yourself

Guest satisfaction is the main goal of all hotels and motels. But profit also plays a part. 1) Who is in charge overall of the hotel's finances? 2) What other employees work for the controller? 3) How are employees chosen for jobs in a hotel?

Just for Fun

3

At the Silver Legacy Hotel and Casino in Reno, guests can watch a model of an old gold mill at work and can go down into a tunnel exactly like a gold mine.

Guests at the Opryland Hotel in Nashville, Tennessee, can spend hours strolling through the two botanical gardens *inside* the hotel.

With all the competition among resorts and hotels these days, many are looking to provide special features to draw their guests. It takes talented and creative people to keep customers entertained and impressed.

Hildy, Wildlife Manager

Hildy cares for the animal collection at the Hyatt Regency in Hawaii. The collection features parrots, penguins, swans, flamingos, cranes, peacocks, and ducks. She has to feed them, keep their living areas clean, and make sure that they remain healthy. She also

As a wildlife manager, you can combine your love of animals with the stability of the lodging industry.

conducts tours, answers questions, and arranges photo sessions.

Hildy has had a life-long interest in animals. Her first hotel-related job was as a cook at a lodge. She worked there while taking courses toward a degree in veterinary medicine. When she saw the newspaper ad for a wildlife manager position at the Hyatt, it sounded great. But she didn't think she was qualified. She had never worked with penguins, flamingos, or cranes. But Hildy decided to apply anyway. To her surprise, she got the job.

Hildy works five days a week from 6:00 A.M. until 5:00 P.M. She begins each day by making sure the cranes, flamingos, and swans are where they're supposed to be, since loud noises, like fireworks displays at night, can scare them off.

Next, Hildy and her assistant go to the indoor bird room to transfer the birds that are displayed in the garden lobby to their cages and perches. Before the transfer, they check the birds' wings for feathers that need clipping so they can't fly away. They make sure all the birds are in good health.

Next, Hildy prepares food and vitamins for the outside birds. By noon the meal carts are ready, and the outside birds are fed. Every afternoon she leads a tour of the hotel's animal collection. A one-hour photo session follows where guests can have pictures taken with birds perched on their arms.

Hildy is outside with the animals most of the day. She always seems to have a group of people around her asking questions about the animals. Some people feel they can do anything they want with the birds since they're out in the open. Hildy often has to find tactful ways to ask people to treat the birds respectfully. This is the hardest part of her job.

The best part about the job Hildy says, is the opportunity to work with animals in a beautiful environment. Hildy is doing what she really enjoys—and getting paid for it!

Wildlife Managers

Most full-time wildlife managers with experience and training make between $15,000 and $20,000 a year, depending on the area of the country they work in. They receive good benefits. This often includes health and life insurance, paid holidays, vacations and sick days, maternity leave, bonuses, a uniform, and retirement benefits, too.

Being a hotel wildlife manager is an exciting and challenging job despite the long hours you must spend on your feet outdoors. Although more hotels have begun to include wildlife as an attraction, it still isn't an easy job to come by. If you're interested in this kind of position, you can prepare yourself for the competition. Take public speaking courses. Take science courses, which will help you to communicate with veterinarians. Read any material on wildlife that is available to you. Finally, get as much experience with animals as you can.

Everything Else

There are a number of fun lodging industry positions. For more options, look at a few copies of *Club Industry*. It's a magazine for people who work in *hotel clubs* and *recreational spas.* It has information about all kinds of new employment trends. If you have an area of expertise that can help people relax and have a good time, chances are there's a hotel or resort that could use you.

Questions to Ask Yourself

Resorts appeal to people of all tastes. 1) What sort of resort might you enjoy working at? 2) What sort of job might you do there? 3) Where can you find such a place?

The People At the Top 4

As we've talked about careers in the lodging industry, the word *manager* has come up many times. No matter what area of a hotel, motel, or resort we're talking about, someone has to be in charge. That person is the manager.

As we've seen, many hotel managers work their way up from positions like that of bellhop or front desk clerk. Others attend hotel schools and management trainee programs to enter the industry.

In either case, jobs in management are not reserved only for college graduates. If you're interested in working your way to the top, managing may be a real possibility for you.

Chain of Command

Here's what the management chain of most major hotels looks like:

Hotel managers are in charge of the overall operation of the hotel. It is up to
the manager to see that everything runs smoothly.

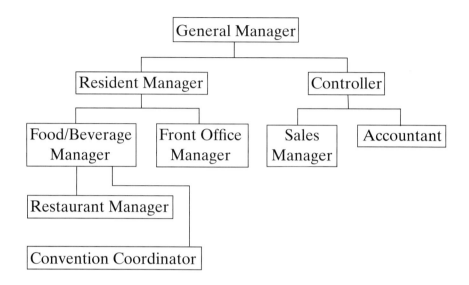

Other managers might be responsible for things like personnel, office administration, marketing, security, recreational facilities, advertising, and public relations.

Do You Have What It Takes?

There is a strong tradition in the lodging industry of rising through the ranks to a top position. But today there are just as many administrators who enter their field in a high-level position to begin with. If *senior-level management,* meaning general manager or resident manager, is your goal, a bachelor's degree in hotel and restaurant administration will be very helpful. More than 150 colleges and universities offer programs in this field.

Over 600 community and junior colleges, technical institutes, and vocational schools also have programs.

Graduates of these programs usually start as *trainee assistant managers* or advance quickly to this position. Then it usually takes five years to rise to a management-level job. The increase in salary ranges from 20 percent to 100 percent.

If you are considering a career in management, but aren't ready for college yet, you can still prepare. Learn how to use a computer. Get experience working in a hotel or motel, even on a part–time basis. Finally, learn about the duties of each type of manager.

General Manager

A *general manager* is responsible for every aspect of the hotel's operation and facilities. He or she directs the management team and decides who's going to be on the management team. A general manager interacts with employees, evaluates their performance, and makes decisions about promotions. He or she also has the final say on the budget and represents the hotel in public affairs.

Resident Manager

A *resident manager* lives in the hotel. He or she is on call twenty-four hours a day to take charge in case of an emergency or sudden problem. He or she reports to the general manager. He or she supervises the housekeeping, room reservations, bell service, and food and beverage departments, as well as the front office and the sales office. A resident manager also handles complaints and is the official host to important guests.

Front Office Manager

A *front office manager* reports to the resident manager and supervises all of the front office personnel and their activities. He or she lets higher management know how many guests are staying in the hotel daily, weekly, monthly, and yearly. A front office manager sets up the filing system for reservation requests, past arrivals, no-show guests, and cancellations. He or she also makes sure guests are handled with courtesy and efficiency, inspects the rooms, and schedules employee work assignments.

A front office manager supervises the front office personnel.

Food and Beverage Manager

A *food and beverage manager* reports to the resident manager and is responsible for all food and beverage services in the hotel. He or she selects the food and beverage products, develops the menu and sets the prices, chooses linens, uniforms, and the decor of the dining room, and selects equipment needed for the kitchen. He or she is also responsible for maintaining customer satisfaction.

Restaurant Manager

A *restaurant manager* reports to the food and beverage manager. He or she hires, trains, and

45

supervises waiters, waitresses, busboys, and captains, and keeps records of personnel performance. He or she also keeps records of restaurant costs and reviews them with the food and beverage manager. The restaurant manager prepares daily statements about the volume of business and makes sure the customer is always satisfied.

Brett, Security Director

Brett's job as director of hotel security at a Hilton Inn is challenging and keeps him on his toes. He is constantly on the lookout for anything out of the ordinary. That includes broken windows, broken locks, or noisy guests. An unfamiliar employee working at the wrong hour or in the wrong place might also catch his attention. He spends most of his working hours walking through the hotel, looking for anything that isn't as it should be.

Sometimes his job calls for calming drunken guests or walking up to people who look suspicious, so Brett is in excellent physical shape, and he knows the right things to say in difficult situations. His strongest talent is avoiding fights, even when people threaten him.

Brett worked in various restaurants when he was in high school, mostly as a busboy. That was the only experience he'd had in the lodging industry, so it took a long interview to convince the manager at the Hilton Inn that he was the right person for the security job. He proved to them that he was physically fit and well-trained in self-defense. The manager put him on a 90-day trial period, during which he took a security course to earn a security certificate issued by the state. After he was hired permanently, Brett also took CPR and first–aid training.

When he was promoted to security director, Brett made sure the three part-time guards he supervises were also in shape and had self-defense, CPR, and first-aid training. None of them wear uniforms or carry guns. If a situation becomes serious, they always call the police or fire department.

The part Brett likes best about his job is the constant variety. Although he can evict people if he thinks it's necessary, his goal is to talk them into behaving. That means a different approach almost every time—from politely asking people to leave to just hanging around until a loud party is over.

Brett's job requires that he remain calm when excitement develops. He has to be able to handle a number of situations at the same time. He also has to know every inch of the hotel, so he studies blueprints and memorizes them and keeps up with insurance and fire codes. Brett works from 7:00 P.M. to 3:00 A.M. with Monday and Tuesday off. He always works weekends because that's when situations that require his attention are most likely to happen.

The salary for *director of hotel security* ranges from $15,000 to $22,000 per year and requires a high school diploma. People with experience in the military or police departments may have a good chance of being hired.

Suzanne, Hotel Catering Coordinator

If you walk into Suzanne's office at a large hotel in Nashville, you will probably find her on the phone booking a musical performance, meeting, or wedding reception. Her job is to organize these events. This involves coordinating the use of the hotel's large ballroom and twelve banquet rooms. It's her responsibility to make sure all arrangements go smoothly for her customers.

Suzanne got her start baking breads and cookies during the Christmas season. That led

It is the responsibility of the hotel's catering coordinator to see that all the details of an event are taken care of.

to requests to do brunches and dinners for as many as 250 people.

Then she was offered a job as an assistant manager at a country club. At the country club, she was constantly in contact with all kinds of service people as well as with many of the guests. This experience prepared Suzanne for her job as hotel catering coordinator.

Suzanne makes events happen the way the customers want them to happen. That involves communicating with the customer, planning in advance, and ordering everything from flowers to table decorations. She deals with tables and chairs, audiovisual equipment, entertainment, *servers, and cleaning crews. It is up to her to make sure the menu is perfect, the room immaculate, and the event on schedule.*

To make all of that happen, Suzanne keeps a schedule book that contains detailed information on the use of every banquet room and ballroom. Each day, she meets with her staff to go over all the events of the following day.

Suzanne spends most of her time talking on the phone, showing people the hotel facilities, selling the hotel's services, booking events, and handling paperwork. The hours are long—sometimes twelve to fourteen a day, starting at 5:30 A.M. The best part is when she is able to pull off an event just the way the customer wants it.

A *hotel catering coordinator* is paid about $30,000 a year.

If you are interested in a job like Suzanne's but you are still in school, you can prepare. Take courses in food preparation. Talk to a catering coordinator at a local restaurant or hotel. And get experience in food service as a waitress or waiter, dishwasher, bus person, or food preparation assistant.

Once you're out of school, you can better your chances by attending a vocational school or earning a college degree. Before you can become the coordinator, you'll need several years of working experience.

Preparation for Management

If jobs in management sound exciting to you, there are several things to remember. You will either need formal education or years of on-the-job training to become a manager. The people who work their way up are committed to the lodging industry. They aren't people who skip from career to career. And finally, even the top managers must have the service attitude. Hyatt Hotels makes sure management keeps in touch with the service attitude by holding an In-Touch Day each year during which Hyatt's top managers work as bellhops, housekeepers, and front desk clerks. If you keep all of these things in mind, you are already taking a step in the right direction.

Questions to Ask Yourself

A major hotel has a long chain of command. 1) Who heads the chain of command? 2) How can you prepare for a job in hotel management?

On Their Own

5

Maybe your dream is to *own* and *run* your own lodging establishment. Usually big hotels are not operated by the people who own them. But many motels and most bed and breakfast inns are run by their owners. These people are called *owner/proprietors*, and they have one of the most demanding and the most rewarding jobs in the lodging industry.

Bev and Sean, Owners

Like most innkeepers, husband and wife team Sean and Bev run the bed and breakfast they own in Rockport. Although the inn's ocean setting gives it the feel of a fairy tale, it takes two people to keep the twelve-room operation going. Keeping guests happy in an old-fashioned country inn involves everything from doing the laundry to keeping up with the bookkeeping.

Bev and Sean are able to do that because of their background. Bev worked summers during high school and college at her grandparents' small resort in Colorado, mostly doing dishes and laundry. In college she majored in history and worked as a bookkeeper to help pay for the tuition. Her first job was at a museum, where she helped to restore old furniture and the building itself. She also learned about marketing techniques and publicity.

Sean's father was a carpenter, so Sean learned how to build or repair almost anything when he was growing up. He was also always interested in sales, from selling candy bars for the fifth grade band to his earning a degree in marketing in college. He was part of the sales team for a large hotel chain when he met Bev. A few years after they were married, they bought a large Victorian house in Rockport.

It took them six months to restore the place. Once the inn opened, they continued to do all the work themselves.

Every day, they fix breakfast for their guests and provide afternoon tea. At the end of the day, they even turn down the beds. In order to make their bed and breakfast inn special, they offer such services as laundry and free bicycles for exploring the area. Together, they work about 105 hours per week.

Owning your own bed and breakfast inn can be as rewarding as it is exhausting.

A typical day starts at 7 A.M. with the preparation of breakfast and the tidying up of the lobby area. There are newspapers to bring in and a flag to raise. Breakfast runs from 8 A.M. to 10 A.M. During that time, Bev and Sean chat with the guests, refill coffee mugs, and answer the phones. At 10 A.M. they clear the tables and check guests out. Their next task is to prepare for incoming guests. Then Sean tackles repairs and maintenance. He also works with the small crew they have now been able to hire while Bev takes reservations on the phone and does paperwork.

At 1 P.M., the three to six new arrivals who appear each day will begin to arrive. Bev and Sean both spend time with new guests to make them feel comfortable. Staying at an inn is very different from lodging at a hotel, so they make an effort to put people at ease. There are also errands, grocery shopping, and banking to do before teatime, which is held at 3:30 P.M. In the evenings, they often handle office projects that can't be done during the busy daytime hours.

The thing they like most about their career is socializing with the guests. They advise them on restaurants and local attractions, especially during breakfast and teatimes. They also enjoy purchasing supplies, from food to antique furniture. Being their own bosses is also very appealing to both of them.

The least fun part, they say, is having to work constantly. They have to do almost everything from changing lightbulbs to fixing leaks. Problems with guests, though they don't come up often, can also be frustrating.

To handle a job like this, an *innkeeper* must enjoy being with people and have a calm approach to all kinds of situations. An innkeeper can't be the type of person who is easily frustrated or needs a lot of privacy. Anyone who wants to travel often or hates pulling weeds or scrubbing floors should look for another line of work. And anyone who can't handle some financial insecurity at first is better off doing something else. There is no regular paycheck, and you never know when there is going to be a slump in the tourist business.

If your dream is to own a small inn or bed and breakfast, start gaining the necessary experience now. Work part-time in a hotel or motel. Get some experience with a general construction contractor. Travel to inns and talk to the owners. Learn about accounting, food preparation, and home decorating by

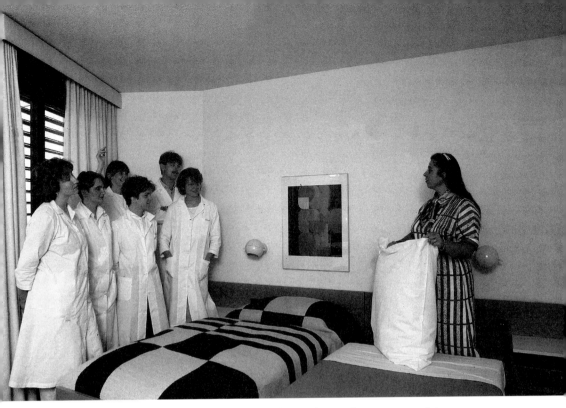

Working in a hotel can give you the training and experience you need to open your own inn.

taking courses or reading about the topic that interests you. If you have the opportunity, work as an apprentice in an inn and learn firsthand.

The benefits of owning and operating your own inn more than make up for the necessary preparation and hard work involved. Being your own employer, hearing the praise of the guests, and earning about $50,000 a year can make it worthwhile.

We've talked about almost every aspect of the lodging industry, from working as a bell-hop to owning your own inn. Turn to the "For

More Information" section to find out where to get more information on your area of interest.

If you decide to pursue a career in hotels, motels, and resorts you are certain to have an exciting and challenging future in a growing industry.

Questions to Ask Yourself

Some people prefer being the owner of a lodging establishment rather than an employee. 1) What is a bed and breakfast inn? 2) Could you handle the responsibility of owning and managing a motel? 3) Would you consider owning and managing a hotel or motel with another person?

Glossary

back–of–the–house The part of the hotel where employees aren't seen by the guests, such as the kitchen.

business office Handles finance, sales, publicity, and personnel.

entry-level Jobs for people with very little training or experience.

front–of–the–house The part of the hotel where employees are seen by the guests, such as the front desk.

human resources The personnel department that deals with the hotel's employees.

lodging industry The business of running hotels, motels, and resorts.

management Highest-level jobs.

owner/proprietor Person who both owns and manages a motel or bed and breakfast inn.

sales and marketing Department that sells what a hotel has to offer.

service attitude Wanting to make guests feel comfortable and satisfied.

For More Information

If you're interested in any of the jobs discussed in this book and would like to know more, you can write to any of the organizations listed here. They will gladly send you information.

American Hotel and Motel Association
1201 New York Avenue NW
Washington, DC 20005
(202) 289-3101

American Management Association
135 West 50th Street
New York, NY 10020
(212) 903-8021

Hotel and Restaurant Employees International Union
1219 28th Street
Washington, DC 20007
(202) 393-4373

National Executive Housekeepers Association
1001 Eastwind Drive
Westerville, OH 43081
(614) 895-7166

If you're interested in running your own hotel or inn, contact the organizations listed below:

Association for Convention Operations Management
c/o William H. Just and Associates, Inc.
1819 Peachtree Street NE
Atlanta, GA 30309
(404) 351-3220

International Association of Hospitality Accountants
Box 27649
Austin, TX 78755
(512) 346-4242

National Federation of Independent Businesses
600 Maryland Avenue SW
Washington, DC 20024
(202) 554-9000

For Further Reading

Henkin, Shepard. *Hotels and Motels.* Lincolnwood, IL: VGM Career Horizons, 1992.

Kennedy, Don. *Careers on Cruise Ships.* New York: Rosen Publishing Group, 1993.

Lattin, Gerald W. *The Lodging and Food Service Industry.* East Lansing, MI: Educational Institute of the American Hotel & Motel Association, 1993.

Managing Front Office Operations. Washington, DC: American Hotel and Motel Association, 1991.

Paige, Grace. *Hotel/Motel Front Desk Personnel.* New York: Van Nostrand Reinhold, 1989.

Schulz, Marjorie Rittenberg. *Hospitality and Recreation.* New York: Van Nostrand Reinhold, 1993.

VNR's Encyclopedia of Hospitality and Tourism. New York, Franklin Watts, 1990.

Index

About the Author
Nancy N. Rue worked for six years as a high school teacher, then turned to free-lance writing. She is the author of several books and more than fifty short stories, articles, and plays. Ms. Rue lives with her husband and daughter in Reno, Nevada.

Photo Credits: Cover, pp. 8, 10, 18, 23, 41 © Hollenbeck Photography/ International Stock; p. 2 © Patti McConville/Image Bank; p. 14 © Schmid Langfield/Image Bank; p. 20 © Bokelbeng/Image Bank; p. 27 © Gordon/Image Bank; p. 36 © Gabe Kircheheimer/Impact Visuals; p. 45 © P & G Bowater/Image Bank; p. 49 © Derek Benwin; p. 54 © Sobel/Klonsky/Image Bank; p. 57 © Brett Froomer/Image Bank.

Design: Erin McKenna